The Tower of Life

HOW YAFFA ELIACH REBUILT HER TOWN IN STORIES AND PHOTOGRAPHS

BY Chana Stiefel   ILLUSTRATED BY Susan Gal

SCHOLASTIC PRESS ✳ ✳ ✳ NEW YORK

There once was a girl named Yaffa.

She was a spirited girl who loved her home and her family.
She was born in a shtetl, a small Jewish town that pulsed
with love, laughter, and light. The name of her shtetl
was Eishyshok (Ay-shi-shok).

The family roots of the people in Eishyshok ran deep. For 900 years, their histories and spirits were woven into the fabric of the town. On holidays, Yaffa's family and their neighbors walked down Eternity Lane to the Old Cemetery, where grandparents told tales of their ancestors buried beneath their feet. Their stories swirled around one another, keeping their faith and traditions alive.

As the seasons turned, Yaffa, her older brother
Yitzchak, and their many cousins played in the town.
In winter, they went sledding and skating.

In summer, they swam in the lake and
chased one another through the forest.

On market days, Yaffa helped her Grandma Chaya sell candles. They laughed as they shouted over the other merchants hawking their wares. An organ-grinder and his pet monkey entertained Yaffa and her friends, handing them fortunes for a fee.

Most of all, Yaffa loved to help out in her Grandma Alte's photography studio just above the family's pharmacy. Many years earlier, Yaffa's grandfather had returned from a visit to America with a brand-new invention: a camera! Since then, Grandma Alte had become one of the town's photographers. She captured the shopkeepers, newlyweds, babies, and bar mitzvah boys on film. It seemed everyone in town wanted Grandma Alte to take their picture!

And on the eve of each Jewish New Year, people from all over Eishyshok would mail their treasured photographs to their families around the world with greetings for good health and happiness.

When Yaffa was six years old, Grandma Alte captured
a treasured moment of Yaffa making funny faces
as she fed the chickens. It seemed the happy
times would never end.

But that same summer, darkness came to Eishyshok.

German tanks and motorcycles rumbled over the
ancient bridge. Boots stomped, hate filled the air.
Jewish schools and businesses were shut down —
including Grandma Alte's photography studio.

Nearly all of the Jews of Eishyshok were
rounded up. Men and women were packed
like cattle inside the town's synagogue.

Sensing doom, Yaffa's father escaped through
one of the synagogue's windows and raced to his
family. He convinced them to flee. They had no time
to collect clothing or food.

But Yaffa tucked a few family photographs into her shoes — special
memories of the life they would leave behind, happiness frozen in time.

In just two days, nearly all 3,500 of Eishyshok's Jewish souls were erased with the hateful explosions of gunfire. Suddenly . . . a deathly silence.

In a heartbeat, 900 years of history — uprooted.

Miraculously, Yaffa, her parents, and her brother Yitzchak escaped to the forest. A kind farmer hid them in his underground shelter. They were cold, hungry, filthy, and frightened. Yaffa held on to her family photographs for dear life.

Over many months, Yaffa's mother taught her to read and write by scraping letters into the damp clay walls of the shelter. Her father kept their spirits alive by sharing stories of the town's holidays and weddings. Yaffa's parents showed her how a glimmer of light can chase away the darkness.

Throughout the war, the family hid in pigsties and potato sheds.
Wherever they ran, Yaffa held on to her precious photographs.
Sunshine and smiles and chickens. They reminded her of home.
Snapshots of light — and life — captured in time.

When the war ended, Yaffa knew it wasn't safe to return to Eishyshok. No Jews remained. As a refugee, she wandered across Europe, through Egypt to Jerusalem.

But Yaffa never let herself be swallowed by the dark past. Instead she worked hard in school, grew up, fell in love, and married.

Yaffa and her husband moved to America and raised a family. Having survived the Holocaust, Yaffa became a professor of history, a world-renowned scholar of that terrible time period.

Every now and then, she looked at her family photographs to remind herself of the life that once was. Her beloved Eishyshok still remained in her heart.

Thirty-five years after the war was over, President Jimmy Carter reached out to Yaffa. A new museum was being built in Washington, DC, documenting the victims of the Holocaust. He asked Yaffa to help build a memorial. But Yaffa didn't want to reflect on death and darkness. Instead she wanted to create something that would shine a light onto the beautiful lives of people lost and forgotten.

But what could that be?

Yaffa thought about Eishyshok's brides and grooms, scholars and schoolchildren, milkmen and musicians. What happened to their families who left before the war? Where did they go? What memories did they hold?

Yaffa remembered the photographs she had tucked in her shoes as a child. That was it! Maybe others saved their photos, too — the family albums they cherished and the pictures they received as New Year's greetings so long ago.

Yaffa decided she would find the survivors and rebuild Eishyshok, not brick by brick, but photograph by photograph, story by story.

Yaffa set off on a sacred mission. She placed ads in newspapers, spoke on radio shows, and followed leads that took her around the globe. She found former residents and descendants of Eishyshok who had stored photographs in attics and basements.

In Israel, Yaffa knocked on 42 doors of an apartment
building until she found a former townsman.
Together they dug up a treasure trove of photos
and letters he had buried in tin cans under
a palm tree.

Whenever she met fellow Eishyshkians, they hugged
and laughed and cried. Many remembered Yaffa as
a child or knew her family. They invited their
family members to revive old stories. Yaffa
felt like she was breathing new life
into her beloved shtetl.

But not everyone trusted
Yaffa with their precious family
photos. Yaffa asked to borrow
albums to make copies. Sometimes
she traded sneakers or color TVs in
exchange for photographs.

And what treasures they were!
The photos showed heroes, not
victims. Dignity, not disaster. Lives
lived, not lost. Every photograph a
world in itself.

In all, Yaffa's journey spanned 17 years. She traveled to six continents, nearly all 50 US states, and hundreds of cities, towns, and villages. She collected 6,000 photographs and stories that included almost every man, woman, and child of Eishyshok's Jewish community from the past 100 years.

Today, if you travel to Washington, DC, you can see Yaffa's "Tower of Life" in the US Holocaust Memorial Museum. More than 1,000 photos of the people of Eishyshok soar three stories high for all the world to see. A world filled with love, laughter, and light — a world that will never be forgotten.

One photograph in the collection shows a curious little girl
in a gingham dress, held in her father's arms.

The girl's name is Yaffa.

She was born in a shtetl called Eishyshok.

May her spirit and legacy continue to shine forever.

A SNAPSHOT OF YAFFA'S LIFE AND LEGACY

1097 ✳ Jews settle in Eishyshok, including ancestors of Yaffa Sonenson Eliach. The region has changed hands many times. During World War II, before it fell to the Germans, it was part of Poland. Today it is known as Eišiškės, Lithuania.

1935 ✳ **May 31.** Yaffa (Shayna) Sonenson is born in Eishyshok.

1941 ✳ **June 23.** Germans invade Eishyshok.
September 21–22. Nearly the entire Jewish population of Eishyshok is rounded up, and Yaffa and her family escape. They flee to the nearby ghetto of Radun, then to the forest, and remain in hiding throughout the war.
September 25–26. Nearly 5,000 Jews from surrounding towns, including 3,446 Jews from Eishyshok, are murdered by *Einsatzgruppen*, mobile killing squads, and buried in mass graves.

1944 ✳ **July.** Eishyshok is liberated by the Russian military.
October 20. Riots break out against Jews. After returning to Eishyshok, Yaffa's mother and baby brother are murdered.

1946 ✳ With her uncle Shalom, Yaffa immigrates to Jerusalem via Europe and Egypt.

1953 ✳ Yaffa marries David Eliach, the principal of the school where she is a student. He immigrates to the United States.

1954 ✳ Yaffa immigrates to the United States to join her husband.

1967 ✳ Yaffa earns a BA in history from Brooklyn College.

1969 ✳ Yaffa earns a master's degree in history from Brooklyn College.

1973 ✳ Yaffa receives her doctorate in history from the City University of New York.

1974 ✳ Yaffa establishes the pioneering Center for Holocaust Studies, Documentation, and Research at Yeshivah of Flatbush in Brooklyn. (The Center has now merged with the Museum of Jewish Heritage.)

1979 ✳ As a member of President Jimmy Carter's Commission on the Holocaust, Yaffa visits former death camps. She vows to return beauty and grace to the victims of the Holocaust by tracking down the descendants of Eishyshok and recording their stories.

1982 ✳ Yaffa publishes *Hasidic Tales of the Holocaust*, 89 stories of Holocaust survivors, which she describes as "a glimmer of hope, a hint of laughter, amid their suffering."

1987 ✳ For the first time since World War II, Yaffa returns to Eishyshok and visits mass graves.

1993 ✳ The United States Holocaust Memorial Museum opens in Washington, DC, featuring the "Tower of Faces," which Yaffa calls the "Tower of Life."

1997 ✳ Yaffa brings 57 people to Eishyshok to hold a memorial service and document the town.

1998 ✴ Yaffa publishes *There Once Was a World: A 900-Year Chronicle of the Shtetl of Eishyshok* (Little, Brown and Company), which becomes a finalist for the National Book Award.

2016 ✴ **November 8.** Yaffa Eliach passes away. She is survived by her husband David (who later passes away in 2021), two children (Rabbi Yotav Eliach and Professor Smadar Rosensweig), 14 grandchildren, and nine great-grandchildren.

The Holocaust was the systematic genocide of European Jews during World War II. Between 1941 and 1945, Nazi Germany and its collaborators murdered approximately six million Jews across Europe, about two thirds of Europe's Jewish population.

BIBLIOGRAPHY

Articles
Berger, Joseph. "Yaffa Eliach, Historian Who Captured Faces of the Holocaust, Dies at 79." *New York Times*, November 9, 2016.
Butler, Menachem. "Yaffa Eliach, the Voice of Hasidic Tales of the Holocaust." *Tablet*, November 15, 2016.
Langer, Emily. "Yaffa Eliach, Holocaust Survivor Who Revived a Lost Town in Photographs, Dies." *Washington Post*, November 10, 2016.
Prial, Frank J. "Coming Out of Hiding: Childhoods as Non-Jews." *New York Times*, May 5, 1991.

Book
Eliach, Yaffa. *There Once Was a World: A 900-Year Chronicle of the Shtetl of Eishyshok*. Little, Brown and Company, 1998.

Photo Archive
https://www.yadvashem.org/archive/about/our-collections/yaffa-eliach/about.html

Videos
Interview with Yaffa Eliach at Miami International Book Festival, 1998. https://youtu.be/h_RRLMPDg6U.
Dr. Yaffa Eliach 2nd Annual Memorial Lecture, Jewish Heritage Museum, NYC. https://www.youtube.com/watch?v=A9x1EvDWPDk&feature=youtu.be.
"There Once Was a Town," narrated by Ed Asner (PBS documentary). https://www.youtube.com/watch?v=ikSdZDwS0s0.

Interviews
Author's interviews with Prof. Smadar Rosensweig, Yaffa's daughter, November 2017; May 17, 2019; April 26, 2021.

FURTHER READING FOR CHILDREN
Elvgren, Jennifer Riesmeyer. *The Whispering Town*. Illustrated by Fabio Santomauro. Kar-ben Publishing, Lerner, 2014.
Hoffman, Amalia. *The Brave Cyclist: The True Story of a Holocaust Hero*. Illustrated by Chiara Fedele. Capstone, 2019.
Hoyt, Megan. *Bartali's Bicycle: The True Story of Gino Bartali*. Illustrated by Iacopo Bruno. HarperCollins, 2021.
Palacio, R.J. *White Bird: A Wonder Story*. Inked by Keven Czap. Alfred A. Knopf, 2019.
Warmflash Rosenbaum, Andria. *Hand in Hand*. Illustrated by Maya Shleifer. Behrman House, 2019.
Wiviott, Meg. *Benno and the Night of Broken Glass*. Illustrated by Josée Bisaillon. Kar-ben Publishing, Lerner, 2010.

EVERY PERSON, A WORLD

Dr. Yaffa Eliach said that when people from all backgrounds visit the "Tower of Life," also known as the "Tower of Faces," at the US Holocaust Memorial Museum, they see the faces of their own family members, even if they have no connection to Eishyshok. That's because the victims of the Holocaust were *people* — human beings who had been leading normal lives. They were not the dehumanized, emaciated prisoners of the Nazi regime. Perhaps that is what drew me toward writing this book: By restoring humanity to the victims, Dr. Eliach exhibited hope and positivity in the face of unbearable pain and tragedy. When I read her obituary in the *New York Times* on November 9, 2016, I felt an instant connection. I knew I had to tell her story.

My mother has always told me that the death toll of the Holocaust was so much more than six million Jews. Each person was a world unto themselves, as illustrator Susan Gal so beautifully depicts. My great-grandfather, Shalom Hershkovitz, who immigrated to America from Czechoslovakia in 1929, lost his parents and eight siblings in the Holocaust, in addition to their spouses and children. Their family trees ended in the hands of the Nazis — a dynasty uprooted, just like the shtetl of Eishyshok. Two of my great-grandfather's siblings survived the Holocaust and, like him, raised Jewish families. My great-grandfather now has more than 300 descendants from his seven children, and the family continues to grow.

Sadly, within the next few years, the last remaining survivors of the Holocaust will be gone. This means that each of us has an even greater responsibility to share their stories. I am grateful to the Eliach and Rosensweig families for giving me permission to share Yaffa's story and help keep her memory alive.

— *Chana Stiefel*

In memory of Dr. Yaffa Eliach, 1935–2016, and the six million Jews who perished in the Holocaust. —*C.S.*

In memory of the children of Eishyshok. —*S.G.*

Special thanks to Yaffa's daughter, Professor Smadar Rosensweig, for her gracious guidance and support, and to Michlean Amir, former longtime librarian and archivist at the United States Holocaust Memorial Museum, for her meticulous fact-checking of this book.

Photos © United States Holocaust Memorial Museum, courtesy of the Shtetl Foundation.

Susan Gal's art was created with ink, watercolor, and digital collage. ✳ The display type was set in KG Hard Candy Solid. ✳ The text type was set in Athelas. ✳ The book was printed and bound in China. ✳ Production was overseen by Lisa Broderick. ✳ Manufacturing was supervised by Irene Chan. ✳ The book was art directed and designed by Marijka Kostiw and edited by Dianne Hess.